W9-AAD-018

EXPLORING SPACE

NASA

by Derek Zobel

Consultant:
Duane Quam, M.S. Physics
Chair, Minnesota State
Academic Science Standards
Writing Committee

BLASTOFF! READERS 3

BELLWETHER MEDIA • MINNEAPOLIS, MN

Note to Librarians, Teachers, and Parents:

Blastoff! Readers are carefully developed by literacy experts and combine standards-based content with developmentally appropriate text.

Level 1 provides the most support through repetition of high-frequency words, light text, predictable sentence patterns, and strong visual support.

Level 2 offers early readers a bit more challenge through varied simple sentences, increased text load, and less repetition of high-frequency words.

Level 3 advances early-fluent readers toward fluency through increased text and concept load, less reliance on visuals, longer sentences, and more literary language.

Level 4 builds reading stamina by providing more text per page, increased use of punctuation, greater variation in sentence patterns, and increasingly challenging vocabulary.

Level 5 encourages children to move from "learning to read" to "reading to learn" by providing even more text, varied writing styles, and less familiar topics.

Whichever book is right for your reader, Blastoff! Readers are the perfect books to build confidence and encourage a love of reading that will last a lifetime!

This edition first published in 2010 by Bellwether Media, Inc.

No part of this publication may be reproduced in whole or in part without written permission of the publisher. For information regarding permission, write to Bellwether Media, Inc., Attention: Permissions Department, 5357 Penn Avenue South, Minneapolis, MN 55419.

Library of Congress Cataloging-in-Publication Data

Zobel, Derek, 1983-
NASA / by Derek Zobel.
    p. cm. – (Blastoff! readers. exploring space)
Includes bibliographical references and index.
Summary: "Introductory text and full-color images explore NASA and its role in space. Intended for students in kindergarten through third grade"–Provided by publisher.
ISBN 978-1-60014-293-2 (hardcover : alk. paper)
1. United States. National Aeronautics and Space Administration–Juvenile literature. 2. Outer space–Exploration–United States–Juvenile literature. 3. Astronautics–United States–Juvenile literature. I. Title.
TL521.312.Z63 2010
629.40973–dc22   2009037959

Text copyright © 2010 by Bellwether Media, Inc.
Printed in the United States of America, North Mankato, MN.

010110   1149

Contents

NASA is a part of the United States government. NASA stands for National **Aeronautics** and Space Administration.

NASA is in charge of space exploration. It was founded in 1958.

Many people work at NASA.
Engineers, scientists, and
astronauts work together
to explore space.

NASA is based in Washington, D.C. Most spacecraft launch from Cape Canaveral, Florida.

In 1957, the **Soviet Union** launched a **satellite** called *Sputnik 1*. This made Americans want the United States to explore space travel too.

Sputnik 1

8

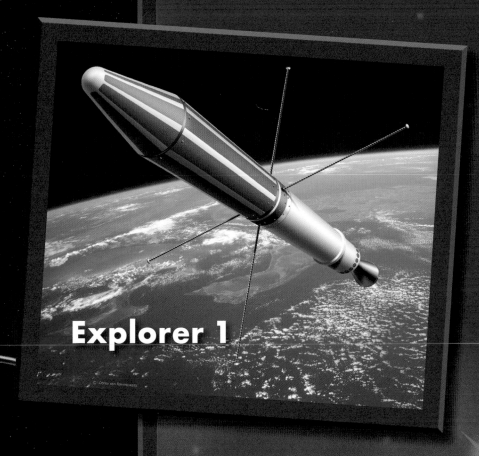

Explorer 1

The United States launched *Explorer 1* in 1958. Soon after, NASA formed. This was the start of the **space race**.

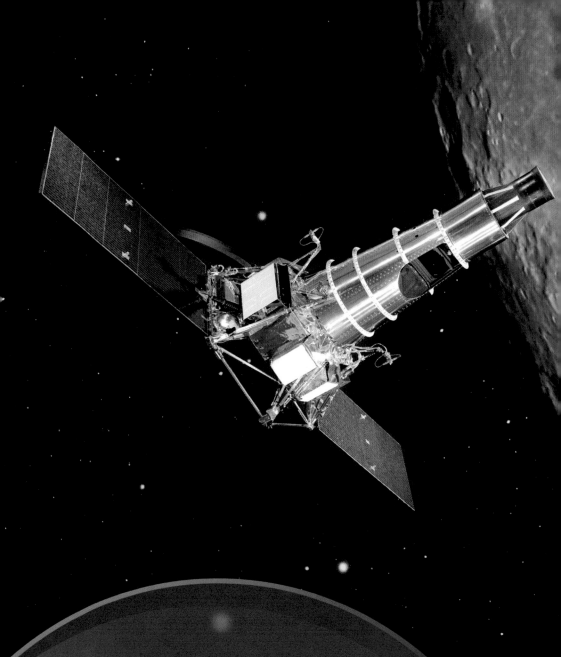

NASA has launched
many **space probes**.

The Surveyor Program sent space probes to the moon to study its surface. It also let NASA practice moon landings.

Mariner 2

The Mariner Program sent space
probes into space to study planets.
Mariner 2 became the first space
probe to fly by another planet.
It passed Venus in 1962.

Mariner 4 flew past Mars in 1965. It sent back photos of the red, rocky surface.

Mariner 4

NASA sent *Voyager 1* and *Voyager 2* into space to study the outer planets.

Voyager 2

Voyager 1 took photos of Jupiter and Saturn. *Voyager 2* explored Uranus and Neptune.

NASA has landed probes on planets. Three **rovers** have landed on Mars.

rover

Scientists and engineers controlled the rovers from Earth.

NASA created the Apollo Program
in 1961. Its goal was to land a man
on the moon. It did this in 1969.

NASA launched the **Hubble Space Telescope** in 1990. It takes incredible images of space objects.

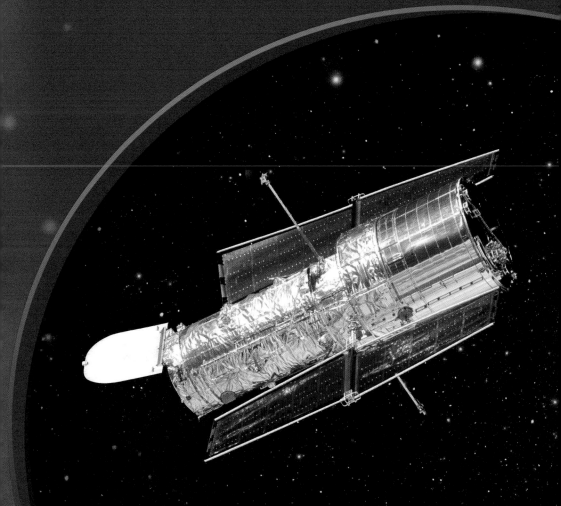

Hubble Space Telescope

NASA uses **space shuttles** to perform space missions. Space shuttles can dock with the **International Space Station.**

International Space Station

NASA works with other countries on this space station. They do experiments to learn more about space.

Glossary

aeronautics—the science of flight

astronauts—people who have been trained to fly aboard a spacecraft and work in space

engineers—people who plan and build machines

Hubble Space Telescope—a telescope that orbits Earth and takes images of space objects

International Space Station—a huge spacecraft built by many countries that orbits Earth; people live on the space station for months at a time; they do experiments and study space.

rovers—probes that land on the surface of a planet and explore to gather information

satellite—an object that is sent into space to orbit Earth; satellites can help predict weather, take pictures of Earth, or beam TV signals to Earth.

Soviet Union—a large country in eastern Europe and western Asia that broke up in 1991; Russia was once part of the Soviet Union and now runs its space program.

space probes—spacecraft that explore planets and other space objects and send information back to Earth; space probes do not carry people.

space race—a race in space technology between the United States and the Soviet Union

space shuttles—spacecraft that carry astronauts into space

To Learn More

AT THE LIBRARY

Cole, Michael D. *NASA Space Vehicles*. Berkeley Heights, N.J.: Enslow Publishers, 2000.

Kortenkamp, Steve. *NASA*. Minneapolis, Minn.: Capstone Press, 2007.

Tocci, Salvatore. *NASA*. New York, N.Y.: Franklin Watts, 2004.

ON THE WEB

Learning more about NASA is as easy as 1, 2, 3.

1. Go to www.factsurfer.com.

2. Enter "NASA" into the search box.

3. Click the "Surf" button and you will see a list of related Web sites.

With factsurfer.com, finding more information is just a click away.

BLASTOFF! JIMMY CHALLENGE

Blastoff! Jimmy is hidden somewhere in this book. Can you find him? If you need help, you can find a hint at the bottom of page 24.

Index

The images in this book are reproduced through the courtesy of: Blakeley / Alamy, front cover, p. 4 (small); NASA, pp. 4-5, 6, 7, 10, 12-13, 17 (small), 16-17, 18, 19, 20-21; Detlev van Ravensway / Photo Researchers, Inc., pp. 8-9, 9 (small); Damian Gil, pp. 10-11; Seth Shostak / Photo Researchers, Inc., pp. 14-15; Photolibrary, p. 20 (small).

Blastoff! Jimmy Challenge (from page 23).
Hint: Go to page 18 and dig in.